D0787156

EUREKA!
I've discovered
Light

Lynette Brent

mc **Marshall Cavendish**
Benchmark

New York

Marshall Cavendish Benchmark
99 White Plains Road
Tarrytown, NY 10591
www.marshallcavendish.us

All Internet addresses were available and accurate when this book went to press.

Library of Congress Cataloging-in-Publication Data
Brent, Lynnette R., 1965-
I've discovered light! / by Lynette Brent.
p. cm. -- (Eureka!)
Includes bibliographical references and index.
ISBN 978-0-7614-3198-5
1. Light--Juvenile literature. I. Title.
QC360.B72 2009
535--dc22
2008014535

Cover : Q2A Media Art Bank
Half Title: Anita Patterson Peppers/ Shutterstock
Terraxplorer/istockphoto: P7; Videowokart/ Shutterstock: P11; vera bogaerts/ Shutterstock:
P15; Andrejs Zavadskis/ Shutterstock: P16; Trutta55/ Shutterstock: P19; Trutta55/
Shutterstock: P19; Johnson Space Center/NASA: P19br; digital file from b&w film copy
neg/ Library of Congress Prints and Photographs Division Washington P19tr; dlewis33/
istockphoto P23; Sheila Terry/ Science Photo Library P24; Mlenny/ istockphoto P27;
Anita Patterson Peppers/ Shutterstock P27tr
Illustrations: Q2A Media Art Bank

Created by Q2AMedia
Creative Director: Simmi Sikka
Series Editor: Jessica Cohn
Art Director: Sudakshina Basu
Designer: Dibakar Acharjee
Illustrators: Amit Tayal, Aadil Ahmed, Rishi Bhardwaj,
Kusum Kala, Pooja Shukla and Sanyogita Lal
Photo research: Sejal Sehgal
Senior Project Manager: Ravneet Kaur
Project Manager: Shekhar Kapur

Printed in Malaysia

1 3 5 6 4 2

Contents

What Is Light?

Look around you. What can you see? Maybe you can see the sky through a window. There might be images flashing on a television or computer screen. You are probably viewing the illustrations on the pages of this book. Yet what, exactly, are you seeing? You are looking at light. In fact, light is all that eyes can really see.

Light travels in waves. That may be hard to imagine, but think about water. When you move your hand through water, you see a wave. Water doesn't move from place to place in that wave. That wave isn't made of water. It is made of energy. Energy travels through water in the form of a wave.

Light waves are made of energy, too. Light has **electrical energy** and **magnetic energy**. That's why another name for light is **electromagnetic radiation**. Radiation is the way light moves. It radiates from its source.

The first person to explain successfully that light moves in waves was Christian Huygens (1629–1695). He was a Dutch scientist with a long list of accomplishments in math, astronomy, and the study of matter and energy. We now know that light can even make waves in a **vacuum**, where there is no air.

Light moves
in waves so fast and small
we cannot see them
with our eyes.

Meet Thomas Young

The Englishman Thomas Young (1773– 1829) proved Huygens's wave **theory** of light. He showed that when light goes through a narrow opening, the light spreads out, so it is not a straight stream. He also proved that the spreading light affected light waves from other sources. This is known as **interference**. This important scientist not only proved properties of light, he advanced the studies of medicine, languages, energy, and mechanics. He even developed a special method of tuning musical instruments.

RIDE THE LIGHT WAVES!

Re-Create Young's Experiment

You Will Need:

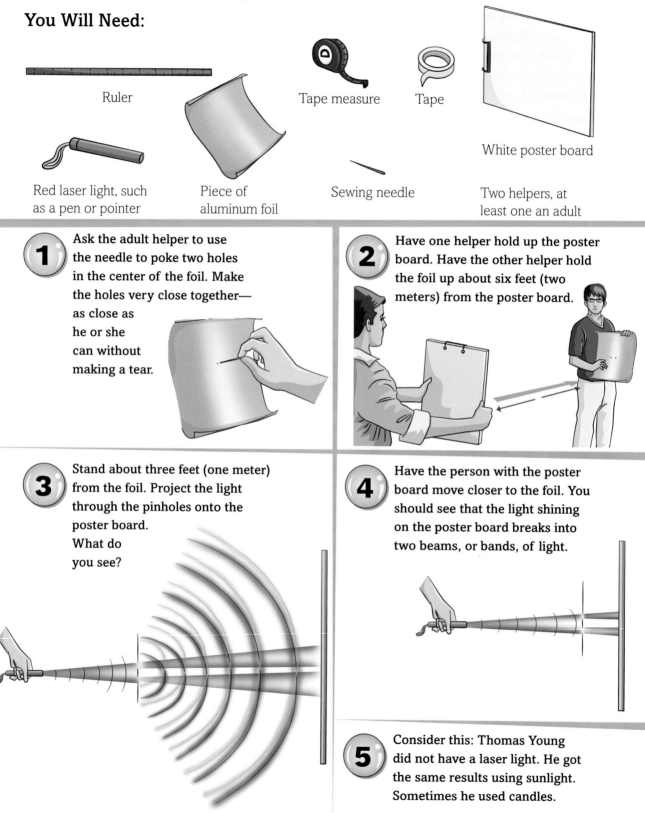

Ruler

Tape measure

Tape

White poster board

Red laser light, such as a pen or pointer

Piece of aluminum foil

Sewing needle

Two helpers, at least one an adult

1 Ask the adult helper to use the needle to poke two holes in the center of the foil. Make the holes very close together— as close as he or she can without making a tear.

2 Have one helper hold up the poster board. Have the other helper hold the foil up about six feet (two meters) from the poster board.

3 Stand about three feet (one meter) from the foil. Project the light through the pinholes onto the poster board. What do you see?

4 Have the person with the poster board move closer to the foil. You should see that the light shining on the poster board breaks into two beams, or bands, of light.

5 Consider this: Thomas Young did not have a laser light. He got the same results using sunlight. Sometimes he used candles.

WHO WOULD HAVE THOUGHT?

A Greek scientist named Euclid wrote *Optica*, a book about light, in about 300 B.C.E. That was three hundred years before the year 1 C.E. Euclid was one of the first scientists to make a link between light and our eyes. From watching light, the ancient Greeks thought of light as streams of **particles**, or very small pieces of things. The Greeks believed that those particles were just too small or too fast to see. Now we believe that light acts like both particles and waves.

The Full Spectrum

Radiation can refer to heat from the Sun or to **nuclear energy**. There are other kinds of radiation, too. They are all part of the **electromagnetic spectrum**. Light we can see is just part of that spectrum:

- Radio waves, which carry signals not only for radio, but also for television and cellphones

- Microwaves, which astronomers use to learn about space (yes, these are the same waves used to cook dinner!)

- Infrared waves, which we experience as heat

- Visible light, the kind you can see

- Ultraviolet light, which comes from the Sun and can damage people's skin

- X-rays, which can be used to look at broken bones

- Gamma rays, the highest energy waves, which can kill living cells!

In 1665, Sir Isaac Newton passed sunlight through a glass **prism**. The light separated into all the colors of the rainbow. Then he placed a second prism next to the first one. He passed light through them both. When the separated light passed through the second prism, the colors recombined. They made one light—white light. That showed that white light had all the other colors of the rainbow: red, orange, yellow, green, blue, indigo, and violet.

White light is many colors combined.

Meet Sir Isaac Newton

Sir Isaac Newton (1642–1727) made many important scientific findings. He showed how the laws of gravity work. He figured out which planets had the most mass and which had the least. How? He used what he knew about gravity and how that force works with bigger and smaller masses. Newton also figured out the speed of sound waves. He was brilliant at math.

FOLLOW THE RAINBOW!

Color Addition

You Will Need:

3 rubber bands

Red, blue, and green cellophane (enough to cover the lens of each flashlight with one color; colored report covers from an office supply store will work, too)

3 flashlights

 1 Use the rubber bands to secure a piece of cellophane to each flashlight. You will need one flashlight covered with red cellophane, one with blue, and one with green.

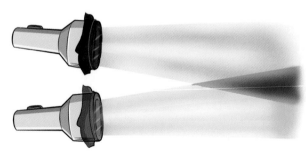

 2 First, shine the flashlight with red cellophane onto a white wall. What color do you see?

 3 Leave the red flashlight on. Now, shine the flashlight covered with blue cellophane. Shine it so the beam of blue light overlaps with the red beam on the white wall. What do you see?

 4 Leave both the red and blue beams of light on the wall. Now shine the flashlight covered with green cellophane on the wall. Shine it so all three beams of light are shining on one spot.

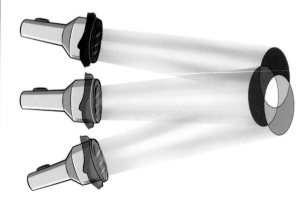

 5 This experiment is like an addition problem. Different colors of light are added together. When the colors red, blue, and green combine, they appear as white light.

WHO WOULD HAVE THOUGHT?

You can see colors on a computer screen, but how do those colors get there? A computer screen contains dots of red, green, and blue. These dots do not glow until an **electronic** beam travels across the screen to create the image. The three colors combine to create the colors you can see on the screen. When blue and red overlap, for example, you see the color magenta. That is a purplish-red. When green and red overlap, you see yellow.

Filled with Light

Objects absorb and reflect light. In other words, they take in some light and some light bounces back. When you see something blue, it is reflecting light rays that make blue light. All the other light rays are absorbed. How does an object absorb light waves? A light wave has a certain **frequency**. Frequency means the number of times a wave passes a certain point in a second. Each light wave has a certain frequency, and its color depends on the frequency.

August Beer was a German scientist. He and the scientist Johann Lambert made an important discovery about light. If Beer could tell the story . . .

Meet August Beer

August Beer (1825–1863) helped establish the Beer-Lambert Law. That law helps us figure out how much light goes through substances. We can use this law to figure out how radiation from the Sun travels through substances in the atmosphere. We can also use this law to explain why different materials absorb light in different ways. The way wood absorbs visible light, we cannot see through wood. Glass is different. The way glass absorbs light waves, we can see through glass.

LIGHT CAN BE FREAKY!

Yes, the absorption of light explains the colors that we see.

There is a relationship between light and the material it travels through.

Leaves of green plants, for example, contain a substance called **chlorophyll**.

Chlorophyll absorbs the blue and red colors of the spectrum and reflect the green.

So, when we look at a plant's leaf, we can see green.

Light Absorption in Black and White

You Will Need:

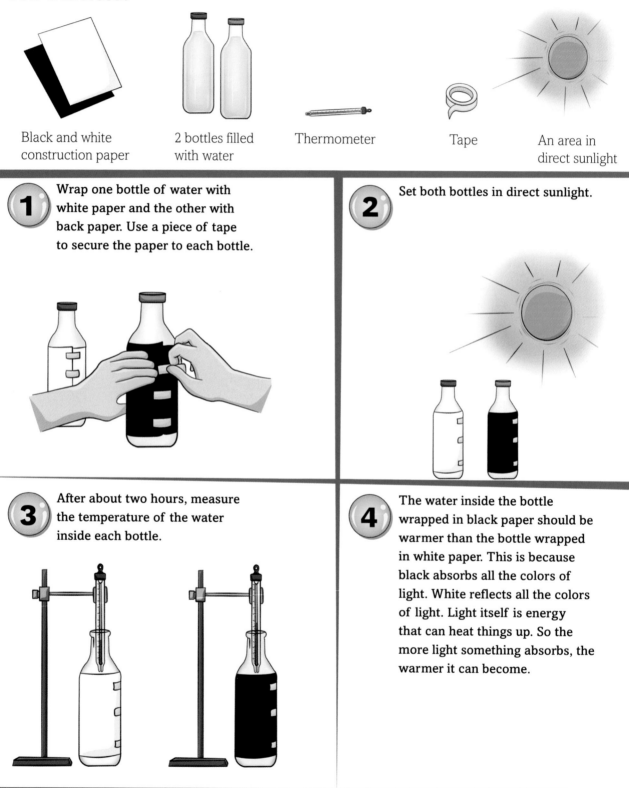

Black and white construction paper

2 bottles filled with water

Thermometer

Tape

An area in direct sunlight

1 Wrap one bottle of water with white paper and the other with back paper. Use a piece of tape to secure the paper to each bottle.

2 Set both bottles in direct sunlight.

3 After about two hours, measure the temperature of the water inside each bottle.

4 The water inside the bottle wrapped in black paper should be warmer than the bottle wrapped in white paper. This is because black absorbs all the colors of light. White reflects all the colors of light. Light itself is energy that can heat things up. So the more light something absorbs, the warmer it can become.

WHO WOULD HAVE THOUGHT?

Earth is surrounded by atmosphere. The atmosphere has gases that act like a greenhouse. These gases are called greenhouse gases. Earth absorbs the sun's light and reflects some of the energy back toward space. Yet the gases trap much of this energy.

We need warmth to survive. If the gases cause Earth to absorb too much light, however, this can cause problems. Over the last one hundred years, Earth warmed by about 1 degree Fahrenheit (about a half degree Celsius). Scientists predict warming will happen more quickly over the next century. Some plants and animals may not be able to adapt quickly enough to survive.

The Ways of Light

Light can act in one of three ways, depending on the material it hits. The first is **reflection**. Some materials do not absorb light. They simply send the energy back from the object. When a wave is reflected off a surface, it comes back at an angle equal to the angle that the wave first hit the surface.

The second is **refraction**. Some materials bend light waves. If light hits a diamond, for example, the waves seem to bend. A rainbow of light can show in the diamond. This happens because the diamond slows down some waves more than others. The waves bend at different angles.

The third is **scattering**. An uneven surface makes light reflect at many angles. The surface of paper is rough, so light scatters when it hits the surface. The waves reflect in all directions.

Scientists such as Hans Lipperhey (about 1570–1619) made scientific advances, using these newer ideas about light. Lipperhey was one of the first to make glass lenses for telescopes.

I can shape glass to shape light.

Meet Zacharias Janssen

Zacharias Janssen (1585–1632) was a Dutch inventor who lived near Hans Lipperhey. The two scientists were in competition. Some historians argue that Janssen was the first to invent the telescope. Some also believe Janssen was first to invent a certain kind of microscope, called the compound microscope. Two things are certain: competition often makes inventors do their best work, and we cannot always say who was first with inventions.

A Glass Filled with Science

You Will Need:

Clear glass

Water

Pencil

1 Fill the glass two-thirds full of water. You can see through water because it is clear, or **transparent**.

2 Place the pencil in the glass and hold it straight up and down. When you look through the side of the glass, the pencil appears straight up and down, just as you are holding it.

3 Let the pencil lean against the side of the glass so that it is entering the water at an angle. When you look at the pencil entering the water at an angle, the pencil appears to be broken. You do not see the pencil as it really is because the light passing through the glass is bending.

4 Light passing through glass slows down slightly. If the light enters the water at an angle, that causes the light beam to bend. It bends away from its original path. This is an example of refraction.

WHO WOULD HAVE THOUGHT?

Why is the sky blue? The sky is blue because Earth's atmosphere is a rough surface. Does this surprise you? We usually think of a surface as something flat that we can touch.

The atmosphere contains different **molecules**, such as **nitrogen**, **oxygen**, and water vapor molecules. These molecules are different sizes. They form an uneven surface.

As light moves through the atmosphere, most of the longer wavelengths pass straight through. Those waves are the reds, oranges, and yellows. Blue light waves are shorter. They are absorbed by the gas molecules. Then they are radiated in all directions in the sky. When you look up, you see reflected blue light. That is why the sky looks blue.

Eyes on the Light

It is hard to see on a dark, moonless night. Your eyes can get used to very little light, but it takes a few minutes. Eyes need light to see.

Your eyes have cells called **rods** and **cones**, named for their shapes. Rods help us see in dim light. Cones operate in bright light. They also allow us to see colors. Rods and cones have cells that create nerve signals, and those signals travel to your brain. So, when you see an object, the signals allow your brain to figure out what you are seeing. Eyes cannot see all types of electromagnetic waves. We are not able, for example, to see microwaves or gamma rays. Rods and cones only detect light in the visible spectrum.

The science of light and sight led to photography. One important figure in photography's history was Louis Jacque Mandé Daguerre. If he could tell his story . . .

Meet Louis Jacque Mandé Daguerre

Louis Jacque Mandé Daguerre (1787–1857) is important in the history of modern photography, although his camera would not seem modern today. He started out as an **apprentice** to an architect. Yet by age sixteen, he was working in theaters, where he became famous for his set and lighting designs. He enjoyed painting pictures, too. His interest in the arts and beautiful images led to his role in photography.

LIGHT IS ALL SHOW!

In 1835, it happened. My assistant and I had been experimenting with silver plates that worked like mirrors.

We were trying to get images to reflect on them and stay. We were using chemicals to absorb the shades of light.

I put one of the used plates into a cupboard. Several days later, I removed the plate and saw an image on it!

There was a broken thermometer in the cupboard. I figured the mercury in the thermometer had something to do with it.

So we experimented with different chemicals. In a couple of years I came up with the **daguerreotype**, a very early kind of photograph.

Wouldn't you know it? The same process had been patented in England only five days before I applied for a patent!

Now You See It, Now You Don't

You Will Need:

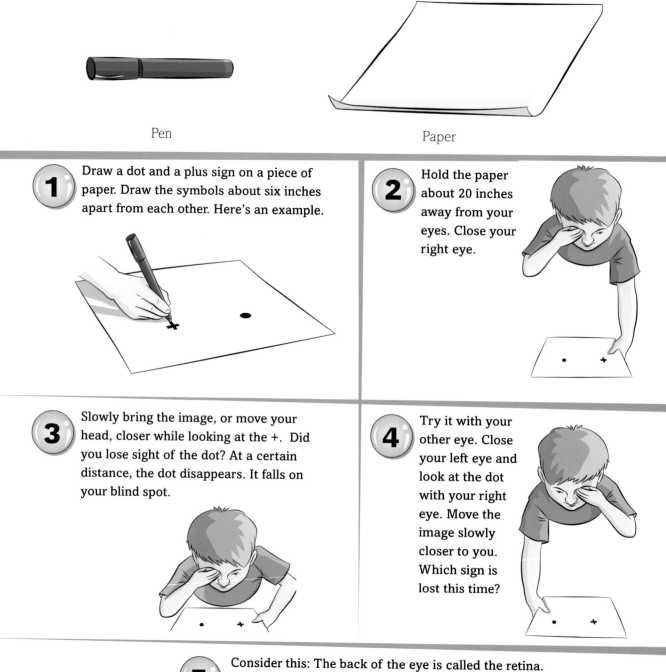

Pen

Paper

1 Draw a dot and a plus sign on a piece of paper. Draw the symbols about six inches apart from each other. Here's an example.

2 Hold the paper about 20 inches away from your eyes. Close your right eye.

3 Slowly bring the image, or move your head, closer while looking at the +. Did you lose sight of the dot? At a certain distance, the dot disappears. It falls on your blind spot.

4 Try it with your other eye. Close your left eye and look at the dot with your right eye. Move the image slowly closer to you. Which sign is lost this time?

5 Consider this: The back of the eye is called the retina. That's where your rods and cones catch light. Those cells send messages about the light to the brain. The messages travel along nerves, which are like wires inside you. Your blind spot is the area of your eye where the nerves meet the retina. There are no rods or cones there!

WHO WOULD HAVE THOUGHT?

People who are **color-blind** have trouble seeing certain colors. The most common form of color-blindness affects the ability to separate the colors red and green. How does this happen? The cones are the cells at the back of the eye that let us see colors. There are cones for red, blue, green, and combinations of the three. If some kinds of cones do not work, it's hard to see some colors. This affects more boys than girls. Out of every twelve boys, usually one is colorblind.

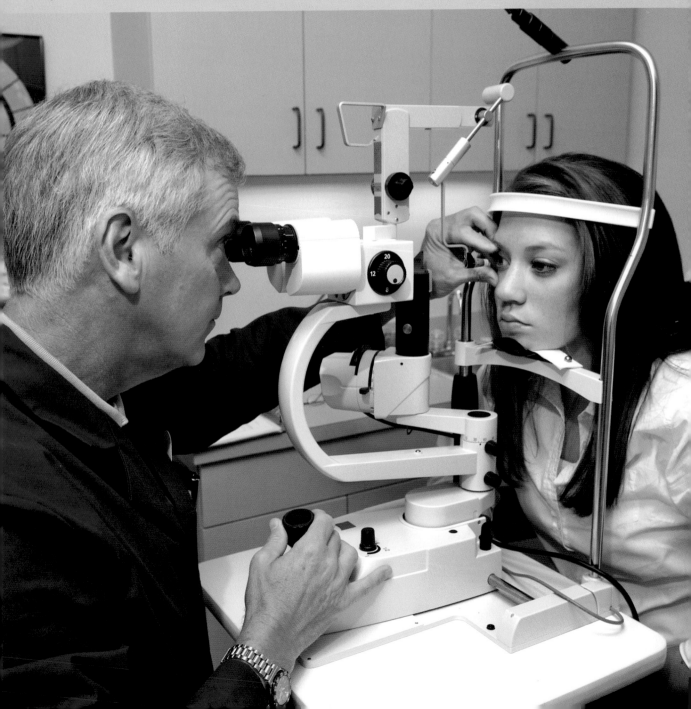

Giving Light

Every time you flip on a light switch, your eyes are exposed to light. You can then take in all the images surrounding you. A light bulb needs electricity to work. Amazingly, today's light bulbs are not that different from the very first bulbs invented.

Inside most light bulbs are two metal contacts. The metal contacts are attached to two wires. The wires are attached to a thin piece of metal called a **filament**. The wires and filament are inside a glass bulb. That bulb is filled with a motionless gas, such as **argon**. Electric current flows from a power supply along one wire. It goes through the filament. It leaves the filament through the other contact and wire.

Lasers are another kind of light. We have many uses for lasers, including cutting patterns in glass or metal. Lasers provide heat in experiments. They even cut into human eyes to correct vision. How do lasers work? Think about what waves look like—they have peaks and valleys. In light from a light bulb, the waves run into each other. In laser lights, however, the peaks and valleys line up. All the waves go in one direction. That makes light from a laser more "orderly" than light from a bulb. Because the light stream is so organized, we can control a laser light better.

The role of gases was important in the design of my lamp and, later, in light bulbs.

Meet Humphry Davy

The British scientist Humphry Davy (1778–1829) led the way to modern light bulbs. In 1815, he invented a safety lamp for use in coal mines. Before that, miners used candles stuck to their helmets. This was dangerous because there were gases in the mines. The gases could explode when they contacted an open flame. Davy was an expert in the science of gases. He discovered that laughing gas could be used to lessen pain during surgery. He also created a process that helped discover new metals.

See What Cannot Be Seen

You Will Need:

2 clear, plastic cups   Tonic water   Tap water   Black paper   Sunlight

1 Label the cups "tonic water" and "tap water." Fill one of the plastic cups with tonic water and the other with tap water. Fill each cup to the brim but don't let them overflow.

2 Set both cups in direct sunlight.

3 Hold the black piece of paper behind the cups in a way that doesn't block the sunlight. Look across the surface of the tonic and tap water through the sides of the cups. What do you see?

4 What happens to the cup of tonic water? What happens to the cup of regular tap water? The tonic water appears to be a glowing blue. The tap water does not have color. Tonic water contains quinine. That substance undergoes change when it absorbs invisible light from the sun. This experiment shows that sunlight is made up of both visible and invisible rays.

WHO WOULD HAVE THOUGHT?

Have you ever seen pictures of fish that glow deep in the ocean? How about fireflies in the night sky? These creatures produce light with a process called **bioluminescence**. Bioluminescence is a chemical reaction. It is the largest source of light in the depths of the oceans. On land, a fungus called foxfire glows the same way. Scientists are studying this natural chemical process to see if we can use it. Some scientists, for instance, hope to line the highways with glowing trees to save electricity. Bioluminescence may be a new chapter in light science.

Timeline

300 B.C.E.
Greek philosopher Euclid publishes *Optica*, a book about light.

1590s
Zacharias Janssen makes a microscope with more than one lens.

1608
Hans Lipperhey applies for a patent for glass lenses that can be used in telescopes.

1609
Galileo is the first to build and use a telescope to study the heavens.

1665
Sir Isaac Newton proves that white light is a mixture of all the colors in the visible spectrum.

1852

August Beer publishes the Beer-Lambert Law, which explains how much light goes through substances.

1830s

Louis Daguerre produces an early version of a photograph.

1815

Humphrey Davy invents a safety lamp, which will lead others to invent light bulbs.

1801

Thomas Young illustrates light interference in an experiment.

1690

Christian Huygens publishes his wave theory of light.

Glossary

apprentice Someone who works for a person who is a master of a certain trade in order to learn the skills of that trade.

argon Colorless, odorless chemical element.

bioluminescence Light given off in certain living things such as fireflies; caused by a chemical reaction.

chlorophyll A pigment in plants that gives them their green color.

color-blind Unable to tell the difference between certain colors.

cone Cell in the eye that is shaped like a cone and helps people see color.

daguerreotype An early photograph produced on a silver or silver-covered copper plate; named for L. J. M. Daguerre.

electrical energy Energy provided by electricity.

electromagnetic radiation Energy in the form of electromagnetic waves.

electromagnetic spectrum Entire range of wavelengths of energy traveling from the Sun to Earth.

electronic Having to do with electrons, the negatively charged particles that orbit around the nucleus of an atom.

filament Thin thread or wire that lights up when heated inside a light bulb.

frequency The number of waves that pass a certain point per second.

interference The meeting of two waves in which the waves cancel each other at some points and strengthen each other at other points.

laser Light with a wavelength that is intense and narrow.

magnetic energy Energy that is contained in a magnetic field.

molecule Smallest particle of a substance that has all the characteristics of that substance.

nitrogen A colorless gas found in numerous forms, including all living material and nearly four-fifths of Earth's atmosphere.

nuclear energy Atomic energy, created by splitting atoms.

oxygen An element found throughout the natural world, including water, most rocks, and as a colorless gas; most organisms need oxygen to live.

particle A tiny unit of matter.

prism Transparent object that bends light so that it breaks up into separate color.

radiation Moving out from a central point.

reflection The return or bouncing back of light or sound waves after striking a surface.

refraction The bending of a ray of light when it passes from one substance into another.

rod Cell in eye that is shaped like a rod and helps people see in dark.

scattering Separating and going in different directions.

theory A reasonable explanation.

transparent Clear; allowing light to pass through.

vacuum Space with no air.

Index